BODY SYSTEMS

SKELETAL SYSTEM

By Simon Rose

MEDIA ENHANCED BOOKS

AV2 BY WEIGL

ADDED VALUE • AUDIO VISUAL

www.av2books.com

AV² provides enriched content that supplements and complements this book. Weigl's AV² books strive to create inspired learning and engage young minds in a total learning experience.

Your AV² Media Enhanced books come alive with...

Audio
Listen to sections of the book read aloud.

Video
Watch informative video clips.

Embedded Weblinks
Gain additional information for research.

Try This!
Complete activities and hands-on experiments.

Key Words
Study vocabulary, and complete a matching word activity.

Quizzes
Test your knowledge.

Slide Show
View images and captions, and prepare a presentation.

... and much, much more!

Go to www.av2books.com, and enter this book's unique code.

BOOK CODE

AVQ67372

AV² by Weigl brings you media enhanced books that support active learning.

Published by AV² by Weigl
350 5th Avenue, 59th Floor
New York, NY 10118
Website: www.av2books.com

Library of Congress Cataloging-in-Publication Data

Names: Rose, Simon, 1961- author.
Title: Skeletal system / Simon Rose.
Description: [2020 edition]. | New York, NY : AV² by Weigl, [2020] | Series: Body systems | Audience: Grades 4 to 6. | Includes index.
Identifiers: LCCN 2018053422 (print) | LCCN 2018059310 (ebook) | ISBN 9781489699336 (Multi User ebook) | ISBN 9781489699343 (Single User ebook) | ISBN 9781489699312 (hardcover : alk. paper) | ISBN 9781489699329 (softcover : alk. paper)
Subjects: LCSH: Human skeleton--Juvenile literature. | Bones--Juvenile literature.
Classification: LCC QP301 (ebook) | LCC QP301 .R655 2020 (print) | DDC 612.7/5--dc23
LC record available at https://lccn.loc.gov/2018053422

Printed in Brainerd, Minnesota, United States
1 2 3 4 5 6 7 8 9 0 22 21 20 19 18

122018
102318

Project Coordinator: Jared Siemens
Art Director: Terry Paulhus

Contents

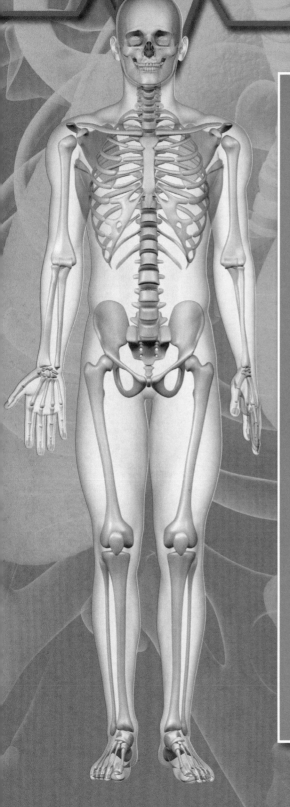

AV² Book Code 2

Human Body Systems.................................... 4

What Is the Skeletal System?...................... 6

Skeletal System Features............................ 8

How Does the Skeletal
System Work?... 10

The Skull... 12

The Spine.. 14

Arms and Hands 16

Legs and Feet.. 18

Keeping Healthy... 20

Timeline... 22

Working Together 24

Careers.. 26

The Skeletal System Quiz........................... 28

Activity 30

Key Words/Index... 31

Log on to www.av2books.com.................... 32

Human Body Systems

The human body is made up of complex systems. There are a total of 11 systems in the body, and 6 main systems. Each one plays an important role in how the body works. The systems are also interconnected. This means they work together.

For the body to stay healthy, its systems need to work together properly. Ensuring that one system is healthy often means that other systems are healthy as well. Weakness or disease in one system can cause problems in one or more of the other systems. The most serious illnesses often affect several of the body's systems.

6 MAJOR BODY SYSTEMS

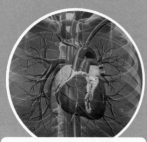

CIRCULATORY SYSTEM

DIGESTIVE SYSTEM

MUSCULAR SYSTEM

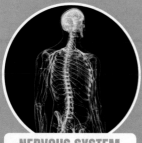

NERVOUS SYSTEM

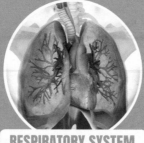

RESPIRATORY SYSTEM

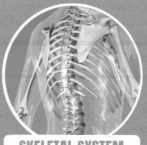

SKELETAL SYSTEM

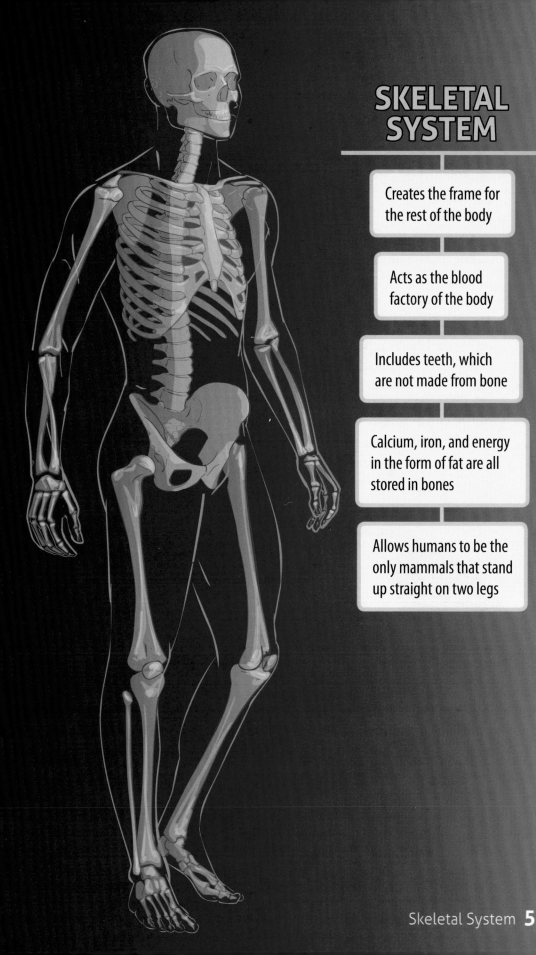

SKELETAL SYSTEM

Creates the frame for the rest of the body

Acts as the blood factory of the body

Includes teeth, which are not made from bone

Calcium, iron, and energy in the form of fat are all stored in bones

Allows humans to be the only mammals that stand up straight on two legs

What Is the Skeletal System?

The skeletal system is a frame that supports the body and gives the body its shape. It includes bones as well as the **cartilage**, **ligaments**, and **tendons** that connect the bones to each other and hold the skeleton together. The skeletal system provides protection and support for the body's internal **organs**. The bones in the skull protect the brain, the bones of the spine protect the spinal cord, and the bones that make up the rib cage protect the heart and lungs.

People have about 300 bones when they are born. As people grow, many of these bones fuse together. By the age of 9 or 10, there are 206 bones in the skeletal system. These bones perform many important functions in the body. Bones are living organs. **Cells** inside human bones work to constantly break down old bone cells and create new cells to keep bones healthy and strong.

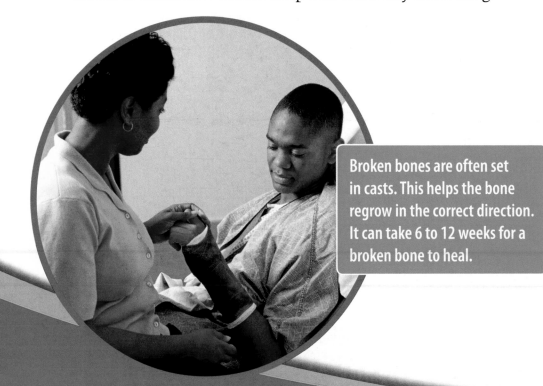

Broken bones are often set in casts. This helps the bone regrow in the correct direction. It can take 6 to 12 weeks for a broken bone to heal.

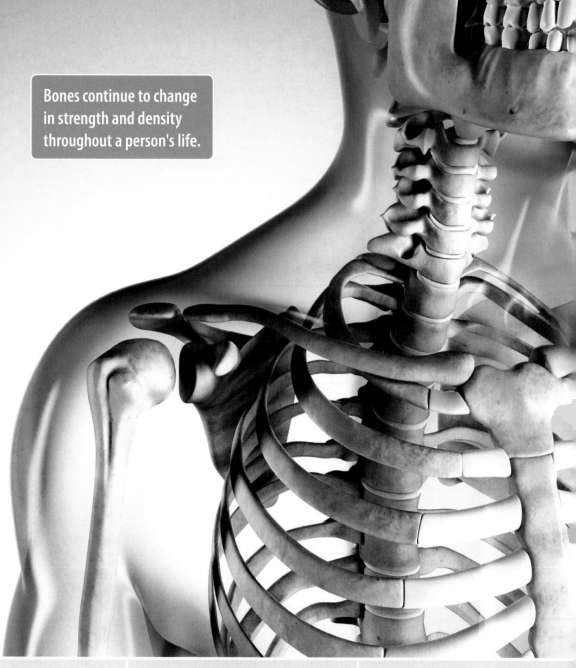

Bones continue to change in strength and density throughout a person's life.

The skeletal system makes up about **20%** of body weight.

The **shortest** bone in the body is the stapes, in the ear. It is only about **0.1 inch** (3 millimeters) long.

Bone is **4 times** as strong as concrete.

Skeletal System Features

The adult skeletal system has two main parts. The axial skeleton has 80 bones, including the skull, **hyoid**, ear bones, ribs, spine, and sternum, or breastbone. The appendicular skeleton contains 126 bones. These include the upper and lower limbs, the pelvis, and the scapula and other shoulder bones.

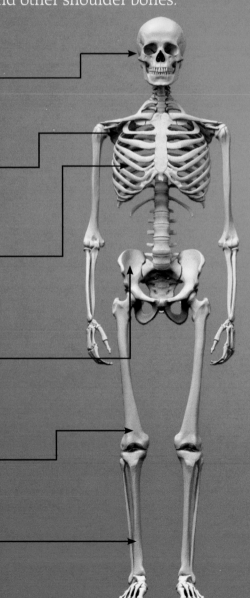

SKULL
These bones are located at the top of the skeleton.

SCAPULA
Also known as the shoulder blade, there is one on each side of the body.

RIBS
The rib cage is formed by 12 pairs of ribs.

PELVIS
This connects the upper bones to the lower limbs and has slight differences between males and females.

FEMUR
This is the largest bone in the human body.

TIBIA
This is the larger of the two bones that make up the lower leg.

SKULL

The exact number of bones that make up the human skull varies depending on how the bones are counted. These bones include those found in the ear and the facial bones that support the eyes, mouth, and nose.

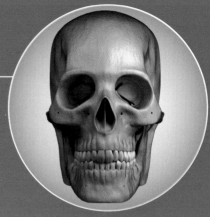

FOOT

The lower leg bones known as the tibia and fibula connect to a large bone called the talus, or anklebone. The big toe has two small bones called phalanges, and the other toes each have three phalanges.

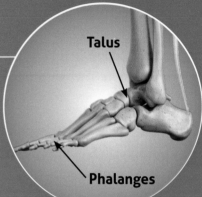

Talus

Phalanges

HAND

The bones of the lower arm connect with a group of eight smaller bones called the carpals to form the wrist joint. The palm of the hand is made up of five bones called metacarpals. The thumb has two bones called phalanges, while the fingers each have three.

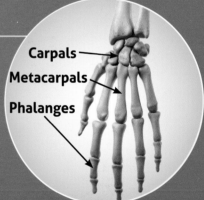

Carpals

Metacarpals

Phalanges

TORSO

The torso is made up of bones that protect and support the heart, lungs, and major blood vessels of the body. The sternum is located in the middle of the chest. It is connected to the upper seven ribs by cartilage. The ribs are also connected to the spine.

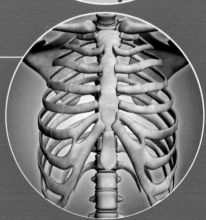

How Does the Skeletal System Work?

People often think of a skeleton as a number of bones connected in the shape of a person. However, bones do not directly connect with one another. They are joined by connective tissues such as cartilage, tendons, and ligaments. Most skeletal muscles work by pulling bones either farther apart or closer together to create movement. The skeletal system's joints bend to allow the bones to move in many different directions.

Blood vessels inside bones provide the skeletal system with nutrients. The skeletal system stores nutrients and **minerals** that are essential to the health of the body. For example, bones store and release calcium into the blood supply when it is needed. Bone cells also release a **hormone** that helps regulate the body's blood sugar and fat deposits.

THE ROLE OF THE SKELETAL SYSTEM

PROTECT
Protects vital organs from damage

PRODUCE
Where the body's blood is made

STORE
Stores and releases minerals that are important to the body

SUPPORT
Supports the other parts of the body

Diagrams of Bone

A bone has a hard and dense outer layer, called compact bone. Beneath this is a layer of spongy bone, which is much lighter and more flexible. In the middle of some bones is a jelly-like substance called bone marrow. There are five types of bones. They are long bones, short bones, flat bones, irregular bones, and sesamoid bones.

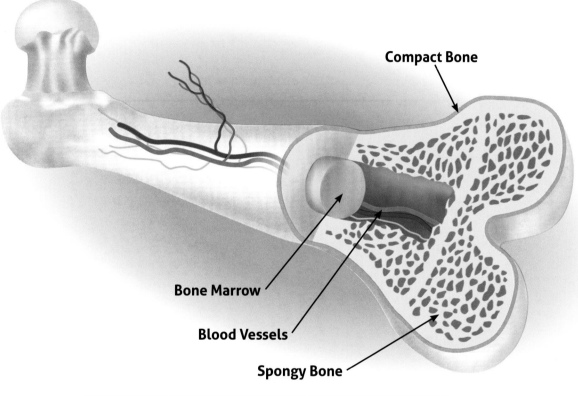

Compact Bone

Bone Marrow

Blood Vessels

Spongy Bone

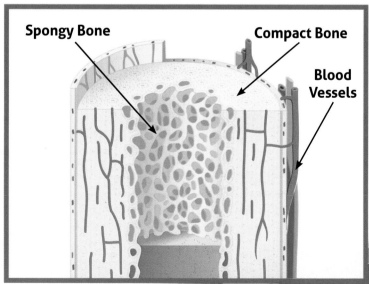

Spongy Bone

Compact Bone

Blood Vessels

The Skull

The skull is located in the top part of the axial skeleton. It is made up of 22 separate bones. The bones at the top of the skull form the cranium, which protects the brain. There are 14 facial bones that support the eyes, mouth, and nose. The bones are fused together by special joints, except for the mandible, or lower jaw. This is the only bone in the skull that is able to move. This allows people to chew food and talk. In children, the fused skull bones remain separate for the first years of life. This allows the brain and skull to grow and develop. The skull bones fuse together at about 2 years of age.

Anchors and Connectors

Other bones in the skull, such as the hyoid bone, anchor muscles in place. In the **middle ear**, three tiny bones connect the eardrum to the inner ear and help with hearing. These bones are the malleus, incus, and stapes.

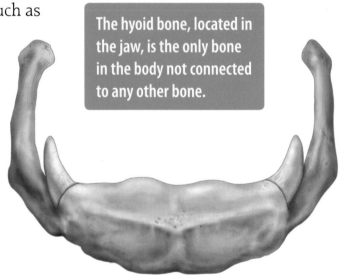

The hyoid bone, located in the jaw, is the only bone in the body not connected to any other bone.

The cranium is made up of **8 bones**.

Children have **20 baby teeth**, which fall out to make space for the adult teeth.

The weight of the average adult head is **10 pounds** (4.5 kg).

10 lb

Diagram of the Skull

The bones of the skull provide protection for vital organs. They also shape the outward appearance of each person's face.

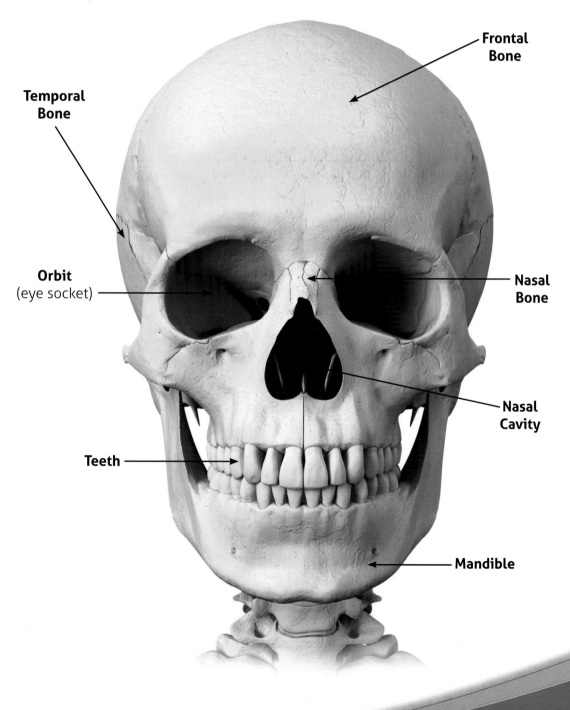

Frontal Bone

Temporal Bone

Orbit (eye socket)

Nasal Bone

Nasal Cavity

Teeth

Mandible

The Spine

The spine is made up of 24 **vertebrae** and two bones made of fused vertebrae. The vertebrae are attached to ligaments and muscles. Between each vertebra, disks made of cartilage serve as a kind of shock absorber to prevent damage to the bones.

Vertebrae

The seven vertebrae at the top of the spine support the head and neck. They are called cervical vertebrae. The first vertebra is called the atlas. It allows the head to move up and down. The second vertebra is called the axis. It allows the head and the atlas to move from side to side.

The 12 thoracic vertebrae are in the upper back. They connect to the ribs to form the rib cage. The five lumbar vertebrae are in the lower back. These bones are very strong because they carry the weight of the upper body. Below the lumbar vertebrae, the sacrum is a single bone made up of five vertebrae fused together. The coccyx, or tailbone, is at the base of the spine. It is a single bone fused from four vertebrae.

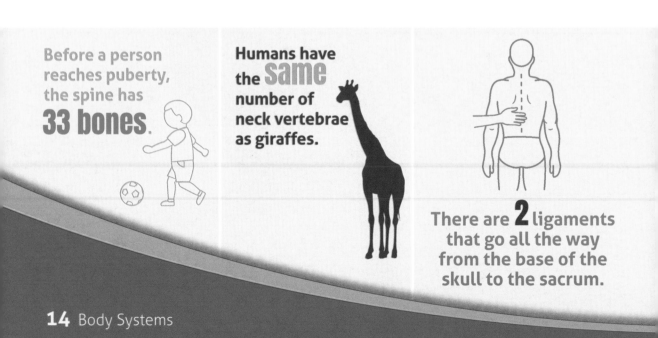

Before a person reaches puberty, the spine has **33 bones**.

Humans have the **same** number of neck vertebrae as giraffes.

There are **2** ligaments that go all the way from the base of the skull to the sacrum.

Diagram of the Spine

With more than 100 joints and 120 muscles, the spine allows a wide range of motion. It also helps hold the body upright.

Spinal Column

There are five different kinds of vertebrae. The main part of each vertebra is called the body. Thin columns of bone extend from the body. These are the spinous process and two transverse processes. Between these and the body is a hollow space that contains the spinal cord and **meninges**.

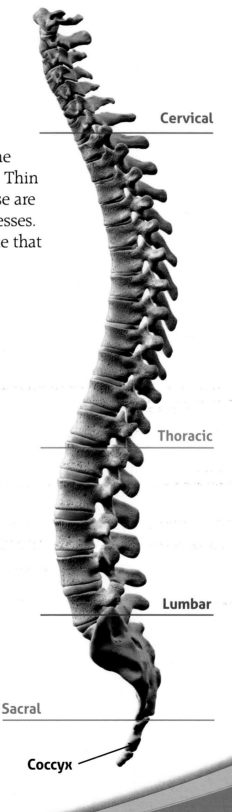

Cervical

Thoracic

Lumbar

Sacral

Coccyx

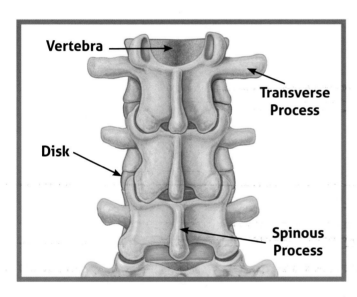

Vertebra

Transverse Process

Disk

Spinous Process

SPINE AND PELVIC BONES

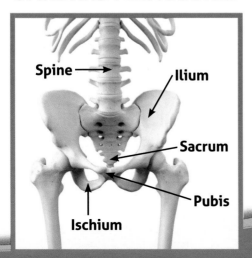

Spine

Ilium

Sacrum

Pubis

Ischium

Arms and Hands

Each arm is attached to a scapula, or shoulder blade. This is a large, triangular bone on each side of the upper back. The upper arm contains the humerus. This bone connects to the scapula with a **ball and socket joint** at the shoulder. It also connects to the bones of the lower arm at the elbow.

The ulna and radius are the bones in the lower arm. They are wider at the ends to give them strength where they meet the joints. At the elbow, the ulna forms a joint with the humerus. The radius is the shorter of the two bones and is on the thumb side of the arm. It allows the hand and forearm to twist at the wrist. Both the ulna and the radius form a joint with the carpals. These small bones allow the wrist to move freely.

The arm and hand bones are connected to tendons and muscles. These tendons and muscles support movement, such as playing a musical instrument.

There are
17 muscles
attached to
the scapula.

Each wrist has
8 joints.

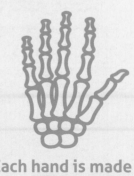

Each hand is made
up of **27 bones**.

Diagrams of the Arm and Hand Bones

The bones in the arms and hands are some of the most used and also the most vulnerable bones in the human body. Arms have some of the most commonly broken bones, making up almost half of all bone injuries in adults.

ARM BONES

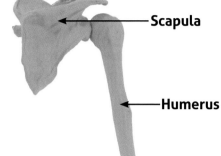

- Scapula
- Humerus
- Elbow Joint
- Radius
- Ulna
- Wrist Joint

Shoulder Joint

The ball-shaped head of the humerus fits into the bowl-shaped end of the scapula at the shoulder joint. This joint allows the arm to move in three different directions.

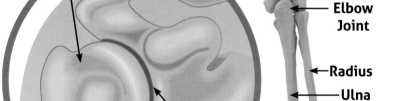

- Ball
- Humerus
- Socket
- Scapula

HAND AND WRIST BONES

- Phalanges
- Metacarpal
- Trapezoid
- Capitate
- Trapezium
- Hamate
- Scaphoid
- Pisiform
- Lunate

Legs and Feet

The left and right hipbones in the pelvic girdle connect the leg bones to the upper part of the skeleton. The femur, or thighbone, connects to the hipbone with a ball and socket joint. It also connects with the tibia and patella, or kneecap, to form the knee joint. The lower leg bones are the tibia and fibula.

The tibia, fibula, and the talus form the ankle joint. The talus is one of the seven tarsal bones located in the foot. The heel bone forms the base of the heel and is attached to the muscles that help the foot to move. The tarsals are seven small bones that make up the back part of the foot and heel.

There are joints between the tarsals and the foot's five long metatarsals. Each of these bones also forms a joint with the small phalanges of the toes. The bones in the foot are arranged to be wide and almost flat, allowing people to stand and walk.

Care for Your Feet

Human feet are not completely flat. The middle part of each foot is arched. Tendons in the feet pull the muscles into an arch. As people age, however, the tendons may become loose. This can result in a condition known as flat feet. To help prevent flat feet, people often wear shoes with arch support.

Diagrams of the Leg and Foot Bones

The bones of the legs and feet help support the entire body. The two largest bones in the body, the femur and tibia, are both in the legs. The femur is also the strongest bone in the body.

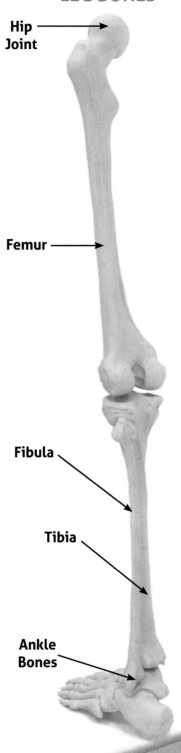

Hip Joint

Femur

Fibula

Tibia

Ankle Bones

KNEE JOINT

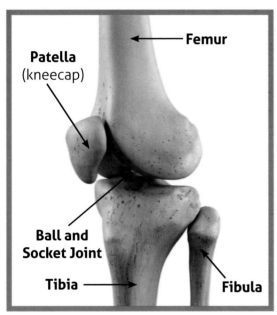

Femur

Patella (kneecap)

Ball and Socket Joint

Tibia

Fibula

FOOT BONES

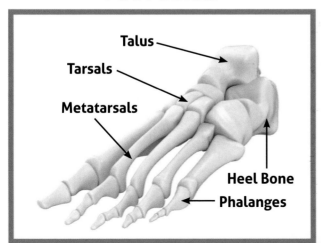

Talus

Tarsals

Metatarsals

Heel Bone

Phalanges

Keeping Healthy

Staying healthy involves regular exercise and eating healthy foods. Calcium and vitamin D help maintain bone health. They can be found in a variety of foods, such as green vegetables.

Exercise

Some of the best ways to maintain healthy bones are weight-bearing exercises, such as jumping rope, running, walking, skiing, and climbing stairs. Maintaining a healthy body weight and lifting weights are other ways to keep bones strong.

Vitamin D

The body needs vitamin D to help it absorb calcium. Vitamin D is found in beef liver, cheese, egg yolks, and in fish such as salmon, mackerel, and tuna. It is often added to milk and cereals as well.

Calcium-Rich Foods

Milk is a source of calcium, but it is not the only one. Calcium is found in other dairy products, such as yogurt and cheese. Leafy green vegetables and fat-rich fish such as salmon also contain calcium. Some grain products, such as breakfast cereals, often have calcium added to them.

FOODS HIGH IN CALCIUM

Yogurt　　Spinach　　Soybeans　　Sardines

Bone Disease

X-rays, bone density tests, and **MRIs** are used to detect diseases and problems in a person's skeletal system.

Osteoporosis is one of the most common bone diseases. It mostly affects older people. This disease causes bones to lose calcium, making them thinner and more likely to break.

Arthritis is a disease that damages the joints and areas around them in many parts of the body. Arthritis usually affects the joints of the hands, hips, knees, lower back, or shoulders. It is most common in older adults, but 300,000 children in the United States have arthritis also.

Scoliosis is a condition that creates a curve in the spine, which looks like a letter "S" or "C" when seen on an X-ray. Most cases are mild and do not need treatment. Some people need to wear a brace or have surgery to straighten their spine.

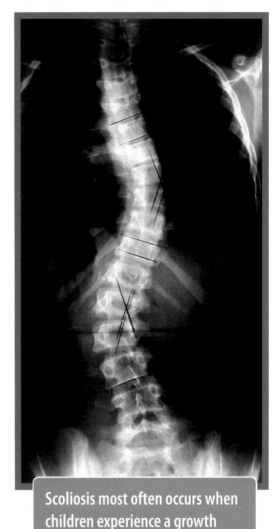

Scoliosis most often occurs when children experience a growth spurt in their early teenage years.

There are
more than 100
different types of arthritis.

About **54 million**
Americans have osteoporosis.

Timeline

Orthopedics is the field of medicine dedicated to the study and treatment of the skeletal system. Today, this is a specialized area of medicine, but people have been studying the human body and skeleton since ancient times.

About 200 AD

Galen of Pergamum is a prominent Greek physician, surgeon, and philosopher. His work influences the practice of medicine throughout Europe until the mid-17th century.

About 400 BC

Considered to be the father of medicine in ancient Greece, Hippocrates wrote about treatment for dislocations of hips, knees, and shoulders, and for infections caused by broken bones piercing the skin.

1600 BC | 400 BC | 250 BC | 100 BC | 50 AD | 200 AD

1600 BC

Anatomy is studied in ancient Egypt. Accounts survive today in the Edwin Smith Surgical Papyrus. It is the oldest known record of medical practices.

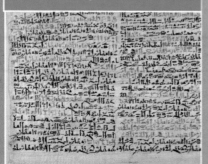

About 300 BC

A school of anatomy is founded in the ancient Egyptian city of Alexandria.

1510

Artist Leonardo da Vinci creates hundreds of drawings in a detailed study of human anatomy, including the skeletal system.

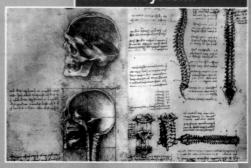

1832

The Anatomy Act in Great Britain makes it easier for doctors to obtain cadavers, or corpses used in medical research.

1970s

Paul Lauterbur makes breakthroughs in developing the MRI. He later wins a Nobel Prize for his work.

2018

Scientists are using 3D printing to create replacement bones and other body parts.

 1500   1650   1800   1950   2100

1895

Wilhelm Roentgen discovers X-rays.

2013

NASA awards $750,000 to scientists to study bone loss in space.

Working Together

No system in the human body works alone. All the systems must work together to keep people healthy and in **equilibrium**. The skeletal system works very closely with other important systems in the body.

Bones and Muscles

The skeletal system works with the muscular and nervous systems to allow the body to move. The ends of every skeletal muscle attach to a bone. The joints in places such as the knee, shoulder, elbow, hip, and neck also work with muscles so that the bones can move.

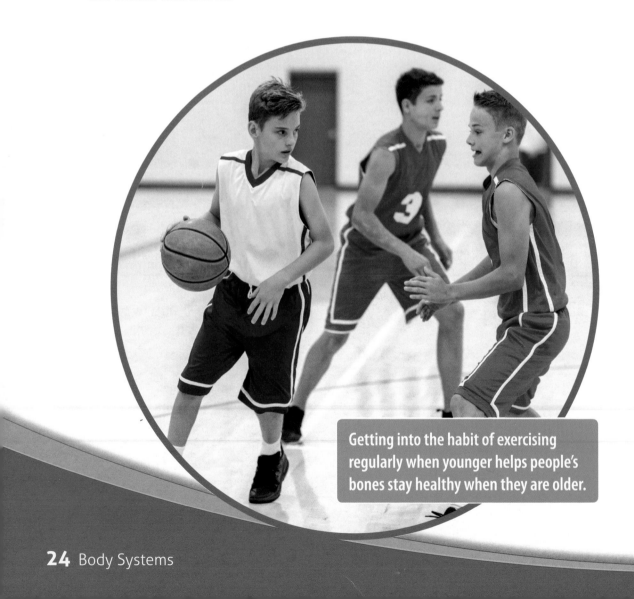

Getting into the habit of exercising regularly when younger helps people's bones stay healthy when they are older.

Making Blood

The skeletal system works with the body's circulatory system to produce and transport blood. Bone marrow contained within the bones produces new blood cells. The circulatory system, which includes the heart and veins, then moves the blood throughout the body. Red blood cells transport oxygen to all parts of the body. White blood cells are part of the body's immune system, which helps protect the body from disease.

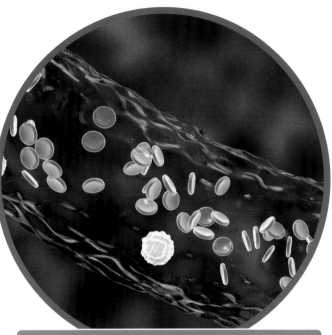

Individual red blood cells survive in the body for about 120 days. The body constantly makes new red blood cells to replace the ones that die.

The skull helps protect a person's brain when an object hits his or her head.

PROTECTING ONE ANOTHER

The bones of the skeletal system protect most of the other body systems. Bones protect the central nervous system from serious damage. The cranium protects the brain, and vertebrae protect the spinal cord. Bones also protect the vital organs of the respiratory system, such as the heart and lungs.

Careers

Some medical careers involve studying or working with the skeletal system. There are many exciting and challenging careers working with technology, research equipment, or treating injuries and disorders related to the skeletal system. Many jobs require a background in biology, physics, or computers. Before considering these careers in healthcare, it is important to research options and learn about the education needed to work in a profession.

X-RAY TECHNICIAN

X-ray technicians use high-tech imaging machines to examine the inside of the body. The pictures they take help doctors to diagnose and treat diseases or injuries more effectively. Some X-ray technicians work with all kinds of patients, while others might specialize in medical conditions affecting specific parts of the body. X-ray technicians work in hospitals, doctor's offices, and specialized medical centers. Radiation is used in their work, so X-ray technicians follow strict safety rules and wear protective clothing when necessary.

Education

- High school degree
- Postsecondary associate's degree in radiography
- Must be licensed (varies by location)

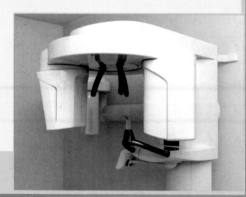

Tool: X-ray Machine

ORTHOPEDIC SURGEON

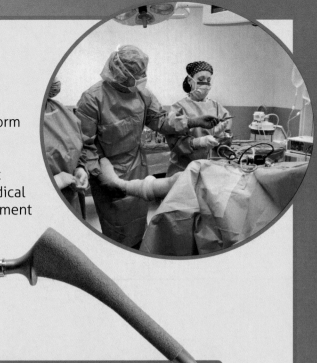

Orthopedic surgeons treat injuries to bones, joints, and muscles. They perform surgery, but they also use physical therapy or treatments, such as casts or splints, to heal injuries. Orthopedic surgeons work closely with other medical professionals to decide the best treatment for a patient.

Education

- Bachelor's degree
- Medical school degree
- Internship and **residency**

Tool: Replacement Hip

PODIATRIST

Podiatrists work with the bones and muscles of the feet, ankles, and legs. They diagnose and treat diseases, injuries, and other issues related to these parts of the body. Podiatrists use tools such as casts and corrective footwear to treat patients. Podiatrists play an important role in preventing foot, ankle, and leg injuries in athletes.

Education

- Bachelor's degree
- Podiatry school
- Residency

Tool: Corrective Footwear

The Skeletal System Quiz

Test your knowledge of the skeletal system by answering these questions. The answers are provided on page 29 for easy reference.

1 What is the largest bone in the human body?

2 How many phalanges does each finger have?

3 How many bones are in the skull?

4 How many bones make up each hand?

5 What acts as a kind of natural shock absorber between each vertebra?

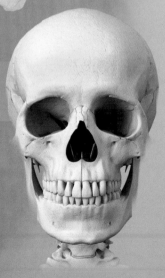

6 What is another name for the scapula?

7 What is the shortest bone in the human body?

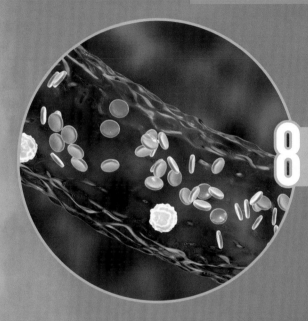

8 What is produced by bone marrow?

9 What vitamin is important for maintaining healthy bones?

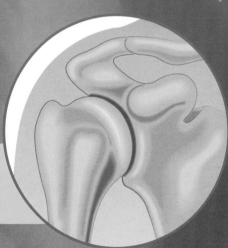

10 What bone disease damages the joints and the areas around them?

Activity

Complete this activity to see how important calcium is in maintaining bone structure and strength.

BEFORE YOU START, YOU WILL NEED:

- 2 clean, dried chicken or turkey leg bones
- 1 large container or jar with a lid
- 2 to 3 cups (0.5 to 0.7 liters) of vinegar

Losing Calcium

1. Make sure your chicken bones are clean and dry. Try to bend them. Are they difficult to bend?

2. Place one bone in the jar, and fill the jar with enough vinegar to cover the bone completely.

3. Put the lid on the jar so it is completely sealed.

4. Put the jar in a safe place where the temperature will not change, and leave your chicken bone to soak in the vinegar for about 4 days.

5. Leave the other bone beside the jar, exposed to open air.

6. Check on the bone in the jar periodically. The calcium carbonate in the bone should be reacting with the mild acid of the vinegar. Look for small bubbles forming inside the jar.

7. On the fourth day, open the jar. Remove the bone from the jar, and dispose of the vinegar.

8. Try to bend the bone now. Has anything changed? How does it compare to the bone that was outside the jar? Why do you think this may be?

Key Words

ball and socket joint: a joint in which the ball-shaped end of a bone fits into a cup-shaped indent of another bone

cartilage: connective tissue found in various parts of the body, such as the joints

cells: the smallest structures of the human body from which all organs and systems are made

equilibrium: a state of total balance

hormone: a substance produced in various organs that helps regulate the body

hyoid: a U-shaped bone in the neck; supports the tongue

ligaments: tissues that either connect to bones or cartilage at a joint, or those that support an organ

meninges: membranes covering the brain and spinal cord

middle ear: the main opening of the ear, separated from the external ear opening by the eardrum

minerals: natural materials the body needs to stay healthy

MRIs: magnetic resonance imaging machines used to produce images of the soft tissues of the body

organs: self-contained parts of the body that serve a particular function

residency: a period, often soon after graduation from medical school, when a doctor receives advanced training by practicing under the supervision of more experienced doctors

tendons: tissues that connect muscle to nearby bones

vertebrae: the bones of the spinal column

X-rays: radiation used to examine the bones inside the body

Index

arthritis 21, 29

bone marrow 11, 25, 29
brain 6, 12, 25

calcium 5, 10, 20, 21, 30
cartilage 6, 9, 10, 14
circulatory system 4, 25

digestive system 4

femur 8, 18, 19, 29

metacarpals 9, 17
metatarsals 18, 19
muscular system 4, 24

nervous system 4, 24, 25

orthopedics 22
orthopedic surgeon 27
osteoporosis 21

patella 18, 19
pelvis 8
phalanges 9, 17, 18, 19, 28
podiatrist 27

respiratory system 4, 25
rib 6, 8, 9, 14

scapula 8, 16, 17, 29
skull 6, 8, 9, 12, 13, 14, 25, 28
spine 6, 8, 9, 14, 15, 21

tibia 8, 9, 18, 19

vertebrae 14, 15, 25, 28
vitamin D 20, 29

X-ray technician 26

Log on to www.av2books.com

AV² by Weigl brings you media enhanced books that support active learning. Go to www.av2books.com, and enter the special code found on page 2 of this book. You will gain access to enriched and enhanced content that supplements and complements this book. Content includes video, audio, weblinks, quizzes, a slide show, and activities.

AV² Online Navigation

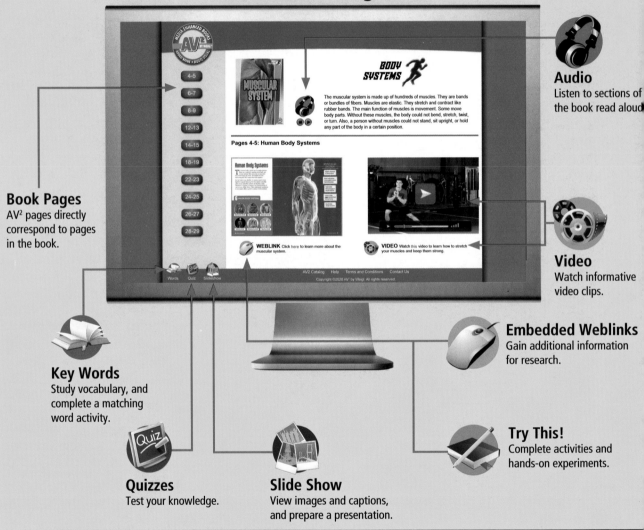

Audio
Listen to sections of the book read aloud

Video
Watch informative video clips.

Book Pages
AV² pages directly correspond to pages in the book.

Embedded Weblinks
Gain additional information for research.

Key Words
Study vocabulary, and complete a matching word activity.

Try This!
Complete activities and hands-on experiments.

Quizzes
Test your knowledge.

Slide Show
View images and captions, and prepare a presentation.

AV² was built to bridge the gap between print and digital. We encourage you to tell us what you like and what you want to see in the future.

Sign up to be an AV² Ambassador at www.av2books.com/ambassador.